CW00495845

Culinary World Tour

Halal Quest and Akusika Cassandra

Published by Halal Quest, 2023.

CULINARY WORLD TOUR

First edition. November 12, 2023.

Copyright © 2023 Halal Quest and Akusika Cassandra.

ISBN: 979-8223269915

Written by Halal Quest and Akusika Cassandra.

Table of Contents

To my parents, who inspired me with their wild imagination and boundless curiosity. This book is dedicated to them with love and thanks for being my biggest fans and my greatest source of inspiration.

To my parents, who instilled in me a love of books and a passion for storytelling. Your unwavering support and encouragement made this dream a reality. Thank you for always believing in me. This book is dedicated to you with all my heart."!

A Global CookBook
Introduction

Welcome to "Culinary World Tour: A Global Cookbook," where we invite you on a delightful journey through the heart and soul of international cuisine. In this culinary adventure, we bring the diverse and delectable flavors of the world straight to your kitchen, turning your cooking experience into a passport-stamped exploration of tastes.

Have you ever craved the comforting aroma of Italian Pasta, dreamt of creating the perfect sushi roll in your own home, or imagined savoring the rich spices of an authentic Indian Curry? This cookbook is your guide to making these culinary dreams a reality.

Each recipe is a page from a global menu, offering not just instructions on how to cook, but a chance to immerse yourself in the cultural tapestry that weaves each dish together. From the iconic Spanish Paella to the American classic Burger, we've gathered a collection that celebrates the art and joy of cooking from every corner of the world.

Whether you're a seasoned chef looking to expand your repertoire or a home cook eager to explore new flavors, "Culinary World Tour" is here to inspire and guide you. Get ready to embark on a culinary expedition that will transport you to different countries, one delicious dish at a time.

So, tie your apron, sharpen your knives, and join us as we embark on a global culinary adventure. Let's make cooking a journey to savor, share, and celebrate the diverse tastes of our world. Bon appétit! ◇◇

Some globally loved dishes include:

1. **Pizza (Italy):** A classic with various toppings.
2. **Sushi (Japan):** Vinegared rice with various ingredients like fish and vegetables.
3. **Tacos (Mexico):** Folded or rolled tortillas filled with various fillings.
4. **Pasta (Italy):** Varied shapes and sauces, like spaghetti with Bolognese.
5. **Curry (India):** Diverse dishes with flavorful spice blends.
6. **Burger (United States):** Ground meat patty in a bun with various toppings.
7. **Dim Sum (China):** Bite-sized portions of dumplings and snacks.
8. **Paella (Spain):** Rice dish with saffron and a mix of seafood or meat.
9. **Croissant (France):** Flaky pastry often enjoyed for breakfast.
10. **Sashimi (Japan):** Thin slices of raw fish, often served with soy sauce and wasabi.
11. **Pad Thai (Thailand):** Stir-fried rice noodles with a combination of ingredients like shrimp, tofu, peanuts, bean sprouts, and lime.
12. **Tiramisu (Italy):** A classic Italian dessert made with layers of coffee-soaked ladyfingers and mascarpone cheese, dusted with cocoa powder.
13. **Chicken Adobo (Philippines):** A Filipino dish where chicken is marinated and simmered in a savory blend of soy sauce,

vinegar, garlic, and spices.

14. **Goulash (Hungary):** A hearty stew made with chunks of beef, onions, paprika, and other spices, often served with noodles or bread.

15. **Moussaka (Greece):** A layered casserole dish with eggplant, minced meat, and béchamel sauce.

16. **Tom Yum Soup (Thailand):** A hot and sour Thai soup usually made with shrimp, mushrooms, lemongrass, lime leaves, and chili.

17. **Pierogi (Poland):** Dumplings filled with various ingredients such as potato, cheese, meat, or sauerkraut, typically boiled or fried.

18. **Rendang (Indonesia):** A rich and flavorful coconut beef stew with a blend of spices, often served with rice.

19. **Ceviche (Peru):** Fresh seafood cured in citrus juices, typically with onions, peppers, and cilantro.

20. **Poutine (Canada):** A Canadian dish consisting of french fries topped with cheese curds and smothered in gravy.

21. **Jollof (Ghana):** A Ghanaian best jollof and we'll recommended by many countries consisting of rice and some ingredients.

These dishes offer a taste of the diverse and delicious offerings from different corners of the world. Enjoy exploring these culinary delights!

Classic Pizza Recipe

Ingredients:

- Pizza dough (store-bought or homemade)

- Tomato sauce

- Mozzarella cheese (fresh or shredded)

- Olive oil

- Toppings of your choice (e.g., pepperoni, mushrooms, bell peppers, olives)

Instructions:

- **Preheat the Oven:**

- Set your oven to the highest temperature it can go (usually around 475-500°F or 245-260°C).

Prepare the Pizza Dough:

- If using store-bought dough, follow the package instructions.

- If making your own, roll out the dough on a floured surface to your desired thickness.

Assemble the Pizza:

- Place the rolled-out dough on a pizza stone or baking sheet.

- Spread a thin layer of tomato sauce evenly over the dough, leaving a small border for the crust.

- Sprinkle a generous amount of mozzarella cheese over the sauce.

Add Toppings:

- Customize your pizza with your favorite toppings. Be creative!

- Some classic choices include pepperoni, sliced bell peppers, mushrooms, and olives.

Drizzle with Olive Oil:

- Lightly drizzle olive oil over the pizza for added flavor and a golden crust.

Bake in the Oven:

- Place the pizza in the preheated oven.

- Bake until the crust is golden and the cheese is bubbly and slightly browned (usually 10-15 minutes, depending on your oven).

Serve and Enjoy:

- Once done, remove the pizza from the oven and let it cool for a few minutes before slicing.

- Serve hot and enjoy your homemade classic pizza!

Sushi Recipe

Ingredients:

- Sushi rice
- Nori (seaweed) sheets
- Fresh fish (e.g., salmon, tuna), thinly sliced
- Vegetables (e.g., cucumber, avocado), thinly sliced
- Soy sauce
- Wasabi and pickled ginger (optional)

For Sushi Rice:

- 2 cups sushi rice
- 1/2 cup rice vinegar
- 1/4 cup sugar
- 1 teaspoon salt

Instructions:
Prepare Sushi Rice:

- Rinse the sushi rice under cold water until the water runs clear.

- Cook the rice according to package instructions.

- While the rice is still hot, mix it with a mixture of rice vinegar, sugar, and salt. Allow it to cool to room temperature.

Prepare Sushi Ingredients:

- Slice the fish and vegetables into thin strips.

- Place a bamboo sushi rolling mat on a clean surface, and put a sheet of nori, shiny side down, on the mat.

Assemble Sushi Rolls:

- Wet your hands to prevent the rice from sticking, and take a handful of sushi rice. Spread it evenly over the nori, leaving a small border at the top.

- Arrange a few slices of fish and vegetables along the bottom edge of the rice.

Roll the Sushi:

- Lift the edge of the bamboo mat closest to you, and tightly roll the nori and rice over the filling.

- Seal the edge with a bit of water.

- Using a sharp knife, wet it to prevent sticking, and slice the roll into bite-sized pieces.

Serve:

- Arrange the sushi on a plate, and serve with soy sauce, wasabi, and pickled ginger on the side.

- Repeat the process with different combinations of fish and vegetables to make a variety of sushi rolls.

Tips:

- Experiment with different fillings and sauces for a variety of sushi options.

- Keep a bowl of water nearby to dip your hands and knife in to prevent sticking.

- Serve sushi immediately for the best taste and texture.

- Enjoy your homemade sushi!

Tacos Recipe

Ingredients:

- Corn or flour tortillas

- Protein of your choice (e.g., seasoned beef, chicken, pork, or beans for a vegetarian option)

- Toppings: Shredded lettuce, diced tomatoes, grated cheese, diced onions, chopped cilantro

- Salsa (store-bought or homemade)

- Sour cream

- Lime wedges

Instructions:
Prepare the Filling:
Protein:

- Cook your chosen protein with desired seasonings until fully cooked. For beef or chicken, you can use taco seasoning for extra flavor.

- If using beans, you can sauté them with onions, garlic, and your favorite spices.

Toppings:

- Prepare the toppings by chopping lettuce, tomatoes, onions, cilantro, and any other preferred toppings.

Warm the Tortillas:
Stovetop:

- Heat a dry skillet over medium heat. Warm each tortilla for about 15-20 seconds on each side until pliable.

Oven:

- Preheat the oven to a low temperature. Wrap the tortillas in aluminum foil and warm them in the oven for about 5-10 minutes.

Assemble Tacos:
Filling:

- Spoon the cooked protein or beans onto the center of each tortilla.

Toppings:

- Add your desired toppings, such as lettuce, tomatoes, cheese, onions, and cilantro.

Salsa and Sour Cream:

- Drizzle salsa over the filling and add a dollop of sour cream.

Lime Wedges:

- Serve with lime wedges on the side for squeezing over the tacos.

Fold or Roll:
Soft Tacos (Folded):

- Fold the tortilla in half, creating a soft taco.

Hard Tacos (Rolled):

- If using hard taco shells, spoon the filling into the shells and arrange them on a serving tray.

Serve:

- Arrange the assembled tacos on a plate.

- Serve immediately, and encourage diners to customize their tacos with additional salsa, sour cream, or lime.

Tips:

- You can add guacamole, hot sauce, or pickled jalapeños for extra flavor.

- Consider offering a variety of protein options for a taco bar experience.

Enjoy your delicious homemade tacos!

Spaghetti Bolognese Recipe

I ngredients:

- 400g spaghetti
- 1 tablespoon olive oil
- 1 onion, finely chopped
- 2 garlic cloves, minced
- 500g ground beef
- 2 carrots, finely diced
- 2 celery stalks, finely diced
- 2 cans (400g each) crushed tomatoes
- 1/2 cup red wine (optional)
- 2 tablespoons tomato paste
- 1 teaspoon dried oregano
- 1 teaspoon dried basil
- Salt and pepper to taste
- Grated Parmesan cheese for serving

Instructions:
1. Cook the Spaghetti:

- Boil a large pot of salted water. Cook the spaghetti according to package instructions until al dente. Drain and set aside.

2. Prepare the Bolognese Sauce:
a. Sauté Aromatics:
- In a large skillet, heat olive oil over medium heat. Add chopped onions and cook until softened.
- Add minced garlic and cook for an additional 30 seconds.
b. Cook Ground Beef:
- Add ground beef to the skillet. Break it apart with a spoon and cook until browned.
c. Add Vegetables:
- Stir in finely diced carrots and celery. Cook until vegetables are softened.
d. Tomatoes and Wine:
- Pour in crushed tomatoes, tomato paste, and red wine (if using). Stir well.
- Season with dried oregano, dried basil, salt, and pepper. Reduce heat to low, cover, and let it simmer for at least 30 minutes to allow flavors to meld.
3. Assemble and Serve:
a. Combine Sauce and Pasta:
- Mix the cooked spaghetti into the Bolognese sauce. Toss until the pasta is well-coated.
b. Serve:
- Dish out the spaghetti with Bolognese onto plates.
- Garnish with grated Parmesan cheese.
4. Enjoy:

-Serve immediately and enjoy your hearty and flavorful Spaghetti Bolognese!

Tips:

- If you prefer a thicker sauce, simmer uncovered for a longer time.

- Adjust seasoning to taste, and feel free to add fresh herbs like basil or parsley for extra freshness.

Buon Appetito!

Chicken Curry Recipe

Ingredients:

- 500g boneless chicken, cut into bite-sized pieces
- 2 tablespoons vegetable oil
- 1 large onion, finely chopped
- 2 tomatoes, pureed
- 3 cloves garlic, minced
- 1-inch ginger, grated
- 2 tablespoons curry powder
- 1 teaspoon ground cumin
- 1 teaspoon ground coriander
- 1/2 teaspoon turmeric powder
- 1/2 teaspoon chili powder (adjust to taste)
- 1/2 teaspoon garam masala
- Salt to taste
- 1 cup coconut milk
- Fresh coriander leaves for garnish

Instructions:
1. Prepare the Chicken:
In a large pot or deep skillet, heat oil over medium heat.
Add chopped onions and sauté until golden brown.
2. Add Aromatics:
Add minced garlic and grated ginger. Sauté for a minute until fragrant.
3. Spice Blend:
Lower the heat and add curry powder, ground cumin, ground coriander, turmeric powder, chili powder, garam masala, and salt. Stir well to create a flavorful spice base.
4. Cook Chicken:
Add chicken pieces to the pot, coating them in the spice mixture. Cook until the chicken is browned on all sides.
5. Tomato Puree:

Pour in the pureed tomatoes, stirring to combine. Cook until th[e] tomatoes break down and the oil starts to separate from the masala.

6. Coconut Milk:

Add coconut milk to the pot, stirring to incorporate. Simmer f[or] 15-20 minutes until the chicken is cooked through and the flavors mel[d]

7. Adjust Seasoning:

Taste and adjust the seasoning as needed. If you prefer more hea[t] add chili powder or garam masala.

8. Garnish and Serve:

Garnish the chicken curry with fresh coriander leaves.

9. Serving Suggestions:

Serve the chicken curry over steamed rice or with naan bread.

Tips:

- Customize the spice levels according to your preference.

- Experiment with adding vegetables like bell peppers or peas for variation.

- You can marinate the chicken in yogurt and spices for added tenderness and flavor.

Enjoy your aromatic and flavorful Chicken Curry!

Classic Burger Recipe

Ingredients:
    For the Patties:

- 1.5 lbs ground beef (80% lean, 20% fat for juicier burgers)
- Salt and pepper to taste
- Optional: Worcestershire sauce for extra flavor

For the Burgers:
4. Burger buns

- Lettuce leaves
- Sliced tomatoes
- Sliced onions
- Pickles
- Cheese slices (American, cheddar, or your choice)
- Ketchup and mustard
- Mayonnaise

Instructions:
1. Prepare the Patties:

- In a large bowl, gently mix the ground beef with salt, pepper, and Worcestershire sauce (if using).

- Divide the mixture into equal portions and shape them into patties. Make an indentation in the center of each patty to prevent it from puffing up during cooking.

2. Cook the Patties:

- Heat a grill or stovetop pan over medium-high heat.

- Cook the patties for about 3-4 minutes per side for medium-rare, or longer to your desired doneness.

- In the last minute of cooking, place a slice of cheese on each patty and cover to melt.

3. Toast the Buns:

- While the patties are cooking, cut the burger buns in half and toast them on the grill or in a toaster until golden.

4. Assemble the Burgers:

- Place a lettuce leaf on the bottom half of each bun.
- Add a cooked patty with melted cheese on top of the lettuce.

5. Add Toppings:

- Layer sliced tomatoes, onions, and pickles on the patties.

6. Condiments:

- Spread ketchup, mustard, and mayonnaise on the top half of the bun.

7. Complete the Burger:

- Place the top half of the bun over the toppings, pressing down gently.

8. Serve:

- Serve the burgers immediately, and enjoy!

Tips:

- Customize toppings to your liking—consider bacon, avocado, or sautéed mushrooms.

- Ensure the patties are well-seasoned for flavor.

- Let the cooked patties rest for a few minutes before assembling to retain juices.

Enjoy your delicious homemade burgers!

Shrimp Dumplings (Har Gow) - Dim Sum Recipe

Ingredients:
For the Dumpling Wrapper:

- 1 cup wheat starch
- 1/4 cup tapioca starch
- 1/2 teaspoon salt
- 3/4 cup boiling water
- 1 tablespoon vegetable oil

For the Shrimp Filling:
6. 200g fresh shrimp, peeled and deveined

- 1/4 cup bamboo shoots, finely chopped
- 1/4 cup water chestnuts, finely chopped
- 2 tablespoons soy sauce
- 1 tablespoon sesame oil
- 1 tablespoon cornstarch
- 1 teaspoon sugar
- 1/2 teaspoon white pepper

Instructions:
1. Prepare the Dumpling Wrapper:
a. Mix Dry Ingredients:
- In a large bowl, combine wheat starch, tapioca starch, and salt.
b. Add Boiling Water:
- Gradually add boiling water while stirring continuously. Mix until it forms a dough.
c. Add Vegetable Oil:
- Incorporate vegetable oil into the dough. Knead until smooth.
d. Divide and Roll:
- Divide the dough into small portions. Roll each portion into a ba
e. Roll Out Wrappers:
- Flatten each ball into a thin, round wrapper using a rolling pin.

2. Prepare the Shrimp Filling:

a. Chop Shrimp:

- Finely chop the fresh shrimp.

b. Mix Filling Ingredients:

- **In a** bowl, mix chopped shrimp with bamboo shoots, water chestnuts, soy sauce, sesame oil, cornstarch, sugar, and white pepper.

3. Assemble and Steam:

a. Fill the Wrappers:

- Place a spoonful of the shrimp filling in the center of each wrapper.

b. Fold Dumplings:

- Fold the wrapper in half to form a half-moon shape. Pleat the edges to seal.

c. Steam Dumplings:

- Arrange the dumplings on a steamer lined with parchment paper.

- Steam for 8-10 minutes until the dumplings are translucent and the filling is cooked.

4. Serve:

a. Dipping Sauce:

- Prepare a dipping sauce with soy sauce, rice vinegar, and a touch of sesame oil.

b. Garnish and Enjoy:

- Garnish the steamed dumplings with chopped green onions or cilantro.

- Serve hot with the dipping sauce.

Tips:

● Work quickly with the dumpling wrappers, as they can dry out.

● You can customize the filling by adding minced ginger or garlic for extra flavor.

Enjoy your homemade Shrimp Dumplings as a delightful dim sum treat!

Seafood Paella Recipe

ngredients:

- 1.5 cups bomba or short-grain rice
- 4 cups chicken broth
- 1/2 teaspoon saffron threads

33

- 1/4 cup olive oil
- 1 onion, finely chopped
- 3 cloves garlic, minced
- 1 red bell pepper, sliced
- 1 tomato, diced
- 1 teaspoon smoked paprika
- 1/2 teaspoon cayenne pepper (optional for heat)
- 1 cup peas
- 1 pound mixed seafood (shrimp, mussels, calamari)
- Salt and pepper to taste
- Lemon wedges for serving

Instructions:

1. Prepare Saffron Broth:

a. Heat Chicken Broth:

- In a small saucepan, heat the chicken broth until it's hot but n‹ boiling.

b. Infuse Saffron:

- Add saffron threads to the hot broth. Let it steep and infuse t‹ flavor.

2. Sauté Aromatics:

a. Heat Olive Oil:

- In a paella pan or a wide, shallow skillet, heat olive oil over mediu‹ heat.

b. Cook Onion and Garlic:

- Sauté chopped onion and minced garlic until softened.

3. Add Vegetables:

a. Bell Pepper and Tomato:

- Add sliced red bell pepper and diced tomato. Cook until vegetabl‹ are tender.

b. Season with Paprika:

- Sprinkle smoked paprika and cayenne pepper (if using). Stir to combine.

4. Cook Rice:

a. Add Rice:

- Stir in the bomba or short-grain rice until it's well-coated with the oil and spices.

b. Pour Saffron Broth:

- Pour the saffron-infused chicken broth into the pan. Season with salt and pepper.

c. Simmer:

- Bring the mixture to a simmer and cook for about 15-20 minutes until the rice is almost cooked.

5. Add Seafood:

a. Arrange Seafood:

- Nestle the mixed seafood (shrimp, mussels, calamari) into the rice.

b. Add Peas:

- Scatter peas over the top. Continue simmering until the seafood is cooked and the rice has a golden crust on the bottom.

6. Finish Cooking:

Monitor the paella, adjusting heat as needed, until the rice has a lightly crispy bottom layer known as "socarrat."

7. Serve:

Remove from heat and let it rest for a few minutes.
Serve with lemon wedges on the side.

Tips:

- Resist the temptation to stir the rice too much once the broth is added; this helps in forming the coveted socarrat.

- Feel free to customize with additional seafood or meats like chicken or rabbit.

● Paella is often cooked and served in the same pan, adding to its rustic charm.

Enjoy your flavorful and vibrant Seafood Paella!

Homemade Croissants Recipe

Ingredients:
For the Dough:

- 1 1/4 cups warm milk
- 2 1/4 teaspoons active dry yeast
- 1/4 cup granulated sugar
- 3 1/2 cups all-purpose flour
- 1 teaspoon salt
- 1 cup unsalted butter, cold

For the Butter Block:

- 7. 1 1/4 cups unsalted butter, cold

For Egg Wash:

- 8. 1 egg

- 1 tablespoon milk

Instructions:
1. Activate Yeast:
a. Mix Ingredients:
- In a bowl, combine warm milk, active dry yeast, and sugar. Let it si
for about 5-10 minutes until it becomes frothy.
2. Make the Dough:
a. Combine Dry Ingredients:
- In a large mixing bowl, combine flour and salt.
b. Incorporate Yeast Mixture:
- Pour the activated yeast mixture into the flour. Mix until it forms
dough.
c. Chill Dough:
- Knead the dough on a floured surface briefly. Wrap it in plast
wrap and refrigerate for at least 1 hour or overnight.

3. Prepare Butter Block:
a. Layer Butter:

- Place the cold butter between two sheets of parchment paper. Roll it out to a rectangle about half the size of the dough.

b. Encase Butter:

- Roll the chilled dough on a floured surface to a larger rectangle. Place the butter layer on one half of the dough, then fold the other half over the butter, encasing it completely.

c. Chill Again:

- Wrap the dough-butter package in plastic wrap and refrigerate for 30 minutes.

4. Create Layers:
a. Roll and Fold:

- Roll out the dough-butter combination into a rectangle. Fold it into thirds like a letter. This completes one "fold."

b. Repeat Folds:

- Repeat this process for a total of three folds. Chill the dough between each set of folds for at least 30 minutes.

5. Shape and Proof:
a. Roll and Cut:

- Roll out the laminated dough to a thickness of about 1/4 inch. Cut it into triangles.

b. Roll into Croissants:

- Roll each triangle from the wider end towards the tip, creating a crescent shape.

c. Proof:

- Place the shaped croissants on a baking sheet, cover with a cloth, and let them proof at room temperature for 1-2 hours, or until they double in size.

6. Bake:
a. Preheat Oven:

- Preheat your oven to 400°F (200°C).

b. Egg Wash:

- Beat an egg with a tablespoon of milk. Brush this egg wash over the tops of the proofed croissants.

c. Bake:

- Bake for 15-20 minutes or until golden brown and flaky.

7. Enjoy:

- Allow the croissants to cool slightly before serving.

Tips:

- Work with cold ingredients to maintain the flakiness of the pastry.

- Patience is key during the folding and chilling steps to create those layers.

- Experiment with fillings like chocolate or almond paste for different variations.

Savor the delightful flakiness of your homemade croissants!

Salmon Sashimi Recipe

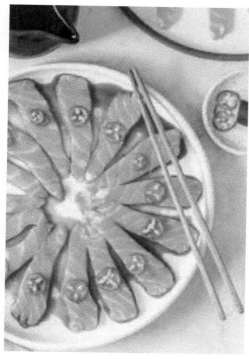

Ingredients:

- Fresh salmon fillet, sushi-grade
- Soy sauce
- Wasabi paste
- Pickled ginger (gari), for serving
- Optional: Sesame seeds and sliced green onions for garnish

Instructions:
1. Choose Quality Salmon:
Purchase sushi-grade salmon from a reputable fishmonger to ensu
freshness and safety for raw consumption.
2. Prepare the Salmon:
a. Skin the Salmon:
- If the salmon fillet has skin, carefully remove it using a sharp knif
b. Slice Thinly:
- Using a very sharp knife, slice the salmon against the grain in
thin, bite-sized pieces. The slices should be about 1/4 inch thick.
c. Arrange on a Plate:
- Arrange the salmon slices on a chilled plate, ensuring they a
evenly spaced.
3. Serve with Accompaniments:
a. Soy Sauce:
- Pour a small amount of high-quality soy sauce into a dipping bow
b. Wasabi:
- Place a small amount of wasabi on the side of the plate. Adjust t
amount according to your preferred level of spiciness.
c. Pickled Ginger:
- Arrange pickled ginger on the plate. This acts as a palate cleans
between bites.
4. Optional Garnish:
Sprinkle sesame seeds and sliced green onions over the salmon f
added flavor and presentation.
5. Serve and Enjoy:
Serve the salmon sashimi immediately, ensuring it is consumed soc
after slicing for the freshest taste and texture.
Tips:

● Freshness is Key: Choose the freshest sushi-grade salmon
available for the best sashimi experience.

● Knife Technique: Use a sharp, long knife and slice the salmon with a single, smooth motion to achieve clean slices.

● Chill the Plate: Place the serving plate in the refrigerator before assembling to keep the sashimi cool.

Enjoy the delicate and delicious flavors of homemade salmon sashimi, a true Japanese delicacy!

Tiramisu Recipe

I ngredients:

- 6 egg yolks
- 3/4 cup granulated sugar
- 1 cup mascarpone cheese, softened
- 1 1/2 cups heavy cream
- 1 cup strong brewed coffee, cooled
- 1/4 cup coffee liqueur (optional)
- 1 package ladyfinger cookies (about 24)
- Unsweetened cocoa powder for dusting

Instructions:

Prepare the Coffee:

- Brew a strong cup of coffee and let it cool. You can add coffee liqueur to the coffee for extra flavor if you like.

Make the Mascarpone Mixture:

- In a large bowl, whisk together egg yolks and sugar until thick and pale.

- Add the mascarpone cheese to the egg mixture and beat until smooth.

Whip the Cream:

- In a separate bowl, whip the heavy cream until stiff peaks form.

- Gently fold the whipped cream into the mascarpone mixture until well combined.

Assemble the Layers:

- Quickly dip each ladyfinger into the brewed coffee (and liqueur if using) and line them in the bottom of a serving dish to create the first layer.

Add the Mascarpone Layer:

- Spread half of the mascarpone mixture over the layer of ladyfingers.

Repeat Layers:

- Create another layer of dipped ladyfingers on top of the mascarpone mixture.

- Add the remaining mascarpone mixture on top.

Chill:

- Cover the dish and refrigerate for at least 4 hours or overnight to allow the flavors to meld.

Dust with Cocoa:

- Before serving, dust the top of the Tiramisu with unsweetened cocoa powder.

Serve:

- Cut into squares or scoop out portions to serve.

Enjoy your homemade Tiramisu!

Pad Thai Recipe

Ingredients:

- 8 oz rice noodles
- 1 cup shrimp, peeled and deveined
- 1 cup tofu, cubed
- 2 eggs, lightly beaten
- 1 cup bean sprouts
- 1/2 cup peanuts, chopped
- 3 green onions, sliced
- 2 cloves garlic, minced
- 1 red chili, finely chopped (optional)
- 2 tablespoons vegetable oil

- Lime wedges for serving

For the Sauce:

- 3 tablespoons fish sauce
- 1 tablespoon tamarind paste
- 1 tablespoon soy sauce
- 1 tablespoon sugar

Instructions:

Prepare Rice Noodles:

Cook rice noodles according to package instructions. Drain and set aside.

Make the Sauce:

- In a bowl, whisk together fish sauce, tamarind paste, soy sauce, and sugar. Set aside.

Stir-Fry Shrimp and Tofu:

- Heat vegetable oil in a wok or large pan over medium-high heat.

- Add shrimp and tofu, stir-frying until shrimp turns pink and tofu is golden brown. Remove from the pan and set aside.

Cook the Eggs:

- In the same pan, add a bit more oil if needed. Pour in the beaten eggs and scramble until just set.

Add Aromatics:

- Push the eggs to one side of the pan and add minced garlic and chopped chili. Stir-fry briefly until fragrant.

Combine Ingredients:

- Add cooked rice noodles to the pan, followed by the prepared sauce. Toss everything together until well combined.

Add Shrimp, Tofu, and Peanuts:

- Return the cooked shrimp and tofu to the pan. Add half of the chopped peanuts and toss to combine.

Finish and Garnish:

- Add bean sprouts and sliced green onions, tossing until they are just cooked but still crisp.

Serve:

- Transfer the Pad Thai to serving plates. Garnish with the remaining chopped peanuts and serve with lime wedges on the side.

Enjoy your homemade Pad Thai!

Chicken Adobo Recipe

I ngredients:

- 2 lbs chicken, cut into serving pieces
- 1 onion, peeled and sliced thinly
- 1 head garlic, peeled and minced
- 1 cup soy sauce
- 1 cup white vinegar
- 1 teaspoon peppercorns
- 3 bay leaves

- 1 tablespoon oil (for cooking)
- 1 cup water
- Salt and pepper to taste
- Steamed rice for serving

Instructions:
Marinate the Chicken:

- In a large bowl, combine chicken pieces, sliced onions, minced garlic, soy sauce, vinegar, peppercorns, and bay leaves. Ensure the chicken is well-coated. Marinate for at least 30 minutes to an hour, or overnight for best results.

Cooking the Chicken:

- In a wide, heavy-bottomed skillet or pot, heat oil over medium heat. Remove the chicken from the marinade, reserving the liquid.

Sear the Chicken:

- Brown the chicken pieces on all sides. This helps to develop flavor. Set aside the onions and garlic from the marinade, but keep the liquid.

Simmer in Marinade:

- Pour the reserved marinade liquid into the pot with the browned chicken. Add 1 cup of water. Bring it to a boil, then reduce the heat to simmer.

Simmer Until Tender:

- Cover and let it simmer for about 30-40 minutes or until the chicken is tender. Stir occasionally.

Adjust Seasoning:

• Taste the sauce and adjust the seasoning with salt and pepper if needed. You can also add more soy sauce or vinegar according to your preference.

Serve:

• Once the chicken is tender and the sauce has reduced to your liking, remove from heat. Discard the bay leaves.

Garnish and Serve:

• Serve Chicken Adobo over steamed rice. Garnish with some chopped green onions or cilantro if desired.

• Chicken Adobo is best enjoyed with its savory sauce over a bed of hot steamed rice. Enjoy your Filipino dish!

Hungarian Goulash Recipe

Ingredients:

- 2 lbs beef stew meat, cut into bite-sized chunks
- 2 large onions, finely chopped
- 3 cloves garlic, minced
- 2 tablespoons vegetable oil
- 2 tablespoons sweet paprika
- 1 teaspoon caraway seeds
- 1 tablespoon tomato paste
- 4 cups beef broth
- 2 bell peppers, diced (optional)
- 2 large potatoes, peeled and diced
- Salt and pepper to taste
- Chopped fresh parsley for garnish
- Noodles or bread for serving

Instructions:
Sear the Beef:

- In a large, heavy pot, heat vegetable oil over medium-high heat. Add the beef chunks and sear on all sides until browned. Remove the beef and set it aside.

Saute Onions and Garlic:

- In the same pot, add chopped onions and garlic. Saute until the onions are softened and translucent.

Add Paprika and Caraway Seeds:

- Stir in sweet paprika and caraway seeds, coating the onions and garlic. Cook for a couple of minutes to release the flavors.

Incorporate Tomato Paste:

- Add tomato paste to the pot and stir well, cooking for another 2 minutes.

Return Beef to Pot:

- Put the seared beef back into the pot, coating it with the onion and spice mixture.

Pour in Beef Broth:

- Pour in the beef broth, ensuring it covers the meat. Bring the mixture to a simmer.

Add Vegetables:

- If using, add diced bell peppers and potatoes to the pot. These add extra flavor and heartiness to the goulash.

Simmer Until Meat is Tender:

- Cover the pot and let the goulash simmer over low heat for 1.5 to 2 hours or until the meat is tender. Stir occasionally.

Adjust Seasoning:

- Season with salt and pepper to taste. Adjust the paprika if more flavor is desired.

Serve:

- Ladle the goulash into bowls and garnish with chopped fresh parsley. Serve with noodles or crusty bread.

- Hungarian Goulash is a comforting and flavorful dish, perfect for colder days. Enjoy!

Moussaka Recipe, a classic Greek dish:

I ngredients:
For the Moussaka:

- 2 large eggplants, sliced into rounds
- **Salt**
- 1/2 cup olive oil
- 1 large onion, finely chopped
- 3 cloves garlic, minced
- 1 lb ground beef or lamb
- 1 can (14 oz) diced tomatoes
- 1/3 cup red wine (optional)

- 1 teaspoon dried oregano
- 1/2 teaspoon cinnamon
- Salt and pepper to taste

For the Béchamel Sauce:

- 4 cups whole milk
- 1/2 cup unsalted butter
- 1/2 cup all-purpose flour
- 1/4 teaspoon nutmeg
- Salt and pepper to taste
- 2 large eggs, beaten

Instructions:
Prepare the Eggplants:

- Slice the eggplants into rounds, sprinkle with salt, and let them sit for about 30 minutes. This helps remove excess moisture and bitterness. Pat them dry.

- Preheat the oven to 400°F (200°C).

- Brush the eggplant slices with olive oil and bake them in a single layer on a baking sheet until golden brown, about 15-20 minutes.

Make the Meat Sauce:

- 4. In a large skillet, heat olive oil over medium heat. Add chopped onions and garlic, sauté until softened.

- Add ground meat, breaking it up with a spoon, and cook until browned.

- Pour in diced tomatoes, red wine (if using), oregano, cinnamon, salt, and pepper. Simmer for about 15-20 minutes until the sauce thickens.

Prepare the Béchamel Sauce:

- 7. In a saucepan, heat the butter over medium heat until melted. Stir in flour and cook for a few minutes to make a roux.

- Gradually whisk in the milk, nutmeg, salt, and pepper. Keep whisking until the sauce thickens, about 10 minutes.

- Remove the saucepan from heat and let it cool slightly. Gradually whisk in the beaten eggs to avoid curdling.

Assemble the Moussaka:

- 10. In a baking dish, layer half of the baked eggplant slices.

- Spread the meat sauce evenly over the eggplant layer.

- Place the remaining eggplant slices on top.

- Pour the béchamel sauce over the top, spreading it evenly.

- Bake in the preheated oven for 45-55 minutes or until the top is golden brown.

- Allow the Moussaka to rest for 15-20 minutes before slicing.

Serve:

- 16. Cut into squares and serve warm. Moussaka is often enjoyed with a side salad and crusty bread.

Enjoy your homemade Moussaka!

Tom Yum Soup Recipe

I ngredients:
   For the Broth:

- 4 cups chicken or vegetable broth
- 2 stalks lemongrass, cut into 2-inch pieces and smashed
- 4 kaffir lime leaves, torn into pieces
- 3-4 slices galangal or ginger
- 2-3 Thai bird's eye chilies, smashed (adjust to taste)
- 3 tablespoons fish sauce
- 1 tablespoon soy sauce (optional)
- 1 tablespoon sugar

- 1 cup mushrooms, sliced (such as straw mushrooms or button mushrooms)

For the Soup:

- 1/2 lb shrimp, peeled and deveined
- 1 medium tomato, cut into wedges
- 1 small onion, sliced
- 2-3 tablespoons lime juice (adjust to taste)
- Fresh cilantro leaves for garnish

Instructions:
Prepare the Broth:

- In a pot, bring the chicken or vegetable broth to a simmer over medium heat.

- Add lemongrass, kaffir lime leaves, galangal or ginger, and smashed Thai bird's eye chilies to the simmering broth.

- Season the broth with fish sauce, soy sauce (if using), and sugar. Let it simmer for about 10-15 minutes to infuse the flavors.

- Add sliced mushrooms to the broth and simmer for an additional 5 minutes.

Add the Soup Ingredients:

- 5. Add peeled and deveined shrimp to the pot. Cook until the shrimp turn pink and opaque.

- Toss in tomato wedges and sliced onions. Cook for another 3-5 minutes until the vegetables are slightly softened.

Adjust Seasoning and Finish:

- 7. Adjust the flavor of the soup by adding lime juice. Taste and adjust the fish sauce or sugar if needed.

- Remove the lemongrass stalks, kaffir lime leaves, and galangal slices from the soup.

Serve:

- 9. Ladle the Tom Yum Soup into bowls, making sure to include shrimp, mushrooms, and vegetables.

Garnish with fresh cilantro leaves.
Enjoy:

- 11. Serve the Tom Yum Soup hot as a delicious and comforting Thai dish. It's often enjoyed as is or with steamed rice.

- This hot and sour Thai soup is packed with vibrant flavors that make it a delightful and comforting choice. Enjoy your homemade Tom Yum Soup!

Pierogi, a traditional Polish dish Recipe

I ngredients:
For the Dough:

- 2 cups all-purpose flour
- 1 large egg
- 1/2 cup sour cream
- 1/4 cup unsalted butter, melted
- 1/2 teaspoon salt

For the Filling:

- Choose one or a combination of the following:
- Mashed potatoes with cheese

- Ground meat (such as beef, pork, or a mixture) seasoned and cooked
- Sauerkraut, drained and sautéed with onions
- Farmer's cheese or a combination of cheeses

For Boiling:

- Salted water

For Frying (Optional):

- Butter or oil for frying

For Serving:

- Sour cream
- Chopped green onions or parsley (optional)

Instructions:
Prepare the Dough:

- In a large bowl, combine flour and salt. Make a well in the center.

- In a separate bowl, whisk together the egg, sour cream, and melted butter.

- Pour the wet ingredients into the well of the dry ingredients. Mix until a dough forms.

- Knead the dough on a floured surface until smooth. Cover with a damp cloth and let it rest for at least 30 minutes.

Prepare the Filling:

● 5. While the dough is resting, prepare your chosen filling(s). Cook and season the meat or sauté sauerkraut with onions, and prepare mashed potatoes or cheese filling.

Assemble the Pierogi:

● 6. Roll out the dough on a floured surface to about 1/8 inch thickness.

● Use a round cutter (about 3 inches in diameter) to cut circles from the dough.

● Place a small spoonful of filling in the center of each circle.

● Fold the dough over the filling to create a half-moon shape. Press the edges to seal, forming a pierogi.

Boil the Pierogi:

● 10. Bring a large pot of salted water to a boil.

● Drop the pierogi into the boiling water in batches. Cook for about 5 minutes or until they float to the surface.

● Remove the pierogi with a slotted spoon and place them on a plate.

Optional: Fry the Pierogi:

● 13. In a skillet, melt butter or heat oil over medium heat.

● Fry boiled pierogi until they are golden brown on both sides.

Serve:

- 15. Serve the pierogi hot with a side of sour cream. Garnish with chopped green onions or parsley if desired.

Enjoy your homemade Pierogi, a delicious and comforting Polish treat!

Rendang, a traditional Indonesian dish Recipe

Ingredients:
For the Spice Paste (Rendang Paste):

- 8-10 dried red chilies, deseeded and soaked in hot water
- 5 shallots, peeled
- 4 cloves garlic, peeled
- 1 thumb-sized ginger, peeled
- 1 thumb-sized galangal, peeled

- 2 lemongrass stalks, white part only, thinly sliced
- 4 kaffir lime leaves, thinly sliced
- 1 teaspoon turmeric powder
- 1 teaspoon coriander powder
- 1/2 teaspoon cumin powder
- 1/2 teaspoon fennel seeds (optional)

For the Rendang:

- 2 lbs beef, cut into cubes (chuck or round roast works well)
- 2 cans (14 oz each) coconut milk
- 2 turmeric leaves, torn (optional)
- 2 kaffir lime leaves
- 2 lemongrass stalks, bruised
- Salt and sugar to taste
- 2 tablespoons tamarind paste (optional, for tanginess)
- Cooking oil

Instructions:
Prepare the Spice Paste:

- In a blender or food processor, combine all the spice paste ingredients. Blend until you get a smooth paste. Set aside.

Cook the Rendang:

- 2. In a large, heavy-bottomed pot or wok, heat a couple of tablespoons of cooking oil over medium heat.

- Add the spice paste to the pot and sauté until fragrant, stirring constantly to prevent burning.

- Add the beef cubes to the pot and cook until they are browned on all sides.

- Pour in the coconut milk, turmeric leaves (if using), kaffir lime leaves, and bruised lemongrass stalks. Stir well.

- Bring the mixture to a boil, then reduce the heat to low. Allow it to simmer uncovered.

- Stir occasionally to prevent the coconut milk from curdling. Continue simmering until the coconut milk thickens, and the beef becomes tender. This process can take 2-3 hours.

- Season with salt and sugar to taste. Add tamarind paste if you prefer a tangy flavor.

- Continue simmering until the coconut milk is fully absorbed, and the beef is coated in a rich, dark brown sauce.

- Once the oil starts to separate from the mixture and the beef is tender, your Rendang is ready.

Serve:

- 11. Serve the Rendang hot with steamed rice or your choice of side dishes.

- Rendang is known for its rich and complex flavors, making it a delightful and savory Indonesian dish. Enjoy your homemade Rendang!

Ceviche, a refreshing Peruvian dish Recipe

Ingredients:

- 1 lb fresh seafood (fish, shrimp, or a combination), diced into bite-sized pieces

- 1 cup fresh lime juice (about 8-10 limes)

- 1 small red onion, thinly sliced

- 1-2 hot peppers (such as jalapeño or serrano), thinly sliced

- 1 bell pepper (red or yellow), diced

- 1 cup cherry tomatoes, halved

- 1/2 cup fresh cilantro, chopped

- Salt and pepper to taste

- 1-2 cloves garlic, minced (optional)

- 1-2 tablespoons extra-virgin olive oil (optional)

- Corn or plantain chips for serving

Instructions:
Prepare the Seafood:

- Ensure the seafood is fresh and of high quality. Use a combination of fish and/or shrimp, and dice them into bite-sized pieces.

- In a glass or stainless steel bowl, combine the seafood with a generous pinch of salt.

- Pour fresh lime juice over the seafood, making sure it's fully submerged. The acidity of the lime juice "cooks" the seafood. Let it marinate in the fridge for about 15-30 minutes, depending on your preference for the level of "cooking."

Prepare the Vegetables:

- 4. While the seafood is marinating, thinly slice the red onion and hot peppers. Dice the bell pepper, halve the cherry tomatoes, and chop the cilantro.

- If you like, add minced garlic to the mix for extra flavor.

- Drain the excess lime juice from the marinated seafood.

Combine Ingredients:

- 7. In a large bowl, combine the marinated seafood with the sliced onions, hot peppers, bell pepper, cherry tomatoes, and cilantro.

- Season the ceviche with salt and pepper to taste. Adjust the level of heat by adding more hot peppers if desired.

- If you like, drizzle extra-virgin olive oil over the ceviche for added richness.

Chill and Serve:

- 10. Cover the ceviche and refrigerate for at least 30 minutes to allow the flavors to meld.

- Serve the ceviche chilled, either in a bowl or individual glasses, accompanied by corn or plantain chips.

- Ceviche is a light and flavorful dish, perfect for warm weather. Enjoy your homemade Peruvian Ceviche!

Poutine, a classic Canadian dish Recipe

I ngredients:
   For the Fries:

- 4 large russet potatoes, peeled and cut into fries
- Vegetable oil for frying

- Salt

For the Gravy:

- 1/4 cup unsalted butter
- 1/4 cup all-purpose flour
- 4 cups beef or chicken broth
- Salt and pepper to taste

For the Cheese Curds:

- 2 cups fresh cheese curds

Instructions:
Prepare the Fries:

- Rinse the peeled and cut potatoes in cold water to remove excess starch.

- Pat the potatoes dry with a kitchen towel.

- Heat vegetable oil in a deep fryer or a large, deep pot to 350°F (175°C).

- Fry the potato strips in batches until golden brown and crispy. Remove with a slotted spoon and place on a paper towel to drain excess oil.

- While the fries are still hot, sprinkle them with salt to taste.

Prepare the Gravy:

- 6. In a saucepan, melt the butter over medium heat.

● Add the flour and whisk continuously to create a roux. Cook for a few minutes until the roux is golden brown.

● Gradually add the broth to the roux, whisking constantly to avoid lumps.

● Bring the mixture to a boil, then reduce the heat and let it simmer until the gravy thickens. Season with salt and pepper to taste.

Assemble the Poutine:

● 10. Place a portion of the hot, crispy fries on a serving plate.

● Sprinkle a generous amount of cheese curds over the fries while they are still hot. The heat from the fries will slightly melt the cheese.

● Pour the hot gravy over the fries and cheese curds, ensuring that the cheese begins to melt and the fries are well-covered.

Serve:

● 13. Serve the Poutine immediately while it's hot, allowing the cheese to melt and the gravy to soak into the fries.

● Poutine is a comforting and indulgent dish that originated in Quebec, Canada. Enjoy your homemade Canadian Poutine!

Ghanaian Jollof Rice Recipe

ngredients:

- 2 cups long-grain parboiled rice
- 1/4 cup vegetable oil

- 1 large onion, finely chopped
- 3 cloves garlic, minced
- 1 tablespoon grated ginger
- 1 can (400g) diced tomatoes or 4 large fresh tomatoes, blended
- 1/2 cup tomato paste
- 1 red bell pepper, finely chopped
- 1 green bell pepper, finely chopped
- 1 teaspoon thyme
- 1 teaspoon curry powder
- 1 teaspoon smoked paprika
- 1 teaspoon cayenne pepper (adjust to taste)
- 4 cups chicken or vegetable broth
- Salt and pepper to taste

Instructions:
Rinse the rice:

- Wash the rice under cold water until the water runs clear. Drain and set aside.

Prepare the sauce:

- In a large pot, heat the vegetable oil over medium heat. Add chopped onions and cook until translucent.

- Add minced garlic and grated ginger, sauté for about a minute until fragrant.

- Stir in the tomato paste and continue to cook for 2-3 minutes.

Add tomatoes and peppers:

• Add the blended tomatoes (or canned tomatoes), red and green bell peppers to the pot. Cook for another 5-7 minutes, stirring occasionally.

Season the sauce:

• Add thyme, curry powder, smoked paprika, cayenne pepper, salt, and pepper. Adjust the seasonings according to your taste.

Simmer:

• Pour in the chicken or vegetable broth and bring the mixture to a simmer. Let it cook for about 10-15 minutes, allowing the flavors to meld.

Cook the rice:

• Add the rinsed rice to the simmering sauce, stirring to ensure the rice is well-coated. Reduce the heat to low, cover the pot, and let it cook until the rice is tender and has absorbed the liquid (about 20-25 minutes).

Check for doneness:

• Occasionally check and stir the rice to prevent sticking. Add more broth or water if needed.

Serve:

• Once the rice is cooked, fluff it with a fork. Serve the Jollof Rice hot, garnished with additional chopped peppers or herbs if desired.

Enjoy your delicious Ghanaian Jollof Rice!

Did you love *Culinary World Tour*? Then you should read *Religions In The World*[1] by Halal Quest!

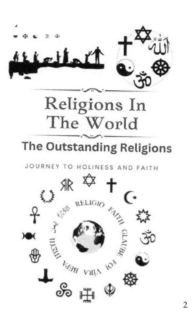

Explore the fascinating diversity of religions around the world in "Religions in the World: The Outstanding Religions." Journey through the beliefs and practices of different faiths, from Christianity and Islam to Buddhism and Hinduism. Discover the stories behind these religions, their key teachings, and how they shape the lives of millions. This easy-to-understand ebook offers a window into the rich understanding of human spirituality, perfect for anyone curious about the world's outstanding religions.

. https://books2read.com/u/3JeB8B

. https://books2read.com/u/3JeB8B

Also by Halal Quest

Quranic Tajweed
Tajweed

Standalone
Religions In The World
The Chrono Guardians
The Magic Of Christmas
Threads Of Deception
Fractured Minds
Culinary World Tour

Also by Akusika Cassandra

Culinary World Tour

Milton Keynes UK
Ingram Content Group UK Ltd.
UKHW040707201123
432908UK00001B/171

9 798223 269916